WESTERN HEROES

Volume 16

Tales of the Wild West Series

Rick Steber

Illustrations by Don Gray

NOTE
WESTERN HEROES is the sixteenth book in
the Tales of the Wild West Series

WESTERN HEROES
Volume 16
Tales of the Wild West Series

Bonanza Publishing
Box 204
Prineville, Oregon 97754

Tales of the Wild West

INTRODUCTION

Buffalo Bill Cody died in 1917 and newspaper headlines around the world proclaimed: *America Loses a Great Western Hero*. Buffalo Bill would have been proud of such a title.

He had been the star of The Buffalo Bill Wild West Show and had brought the western frontier to the doorstep of the world. Wherever he traveled, across the United States or abroad, Buffalo Bill always treated those he met with dignity and respect. He was as comfortable sitting around a campfire with cowboys as he was dining with European royalty. He spoke up for the rights of women and, even though he had fought in the Indian wars, he considered the Indian his equal. He refused to allow the strong to bully the weak and in all instances he made sure justice prevailed.

Although Buffalo Bill is considered to be the ideal role model of the Western Hero many others deserve that title as well. Benjamin Singleton started a movement that brought former slaves to the West. Annie Oakley showed the world that when it came to shooting, a woman could outshoot the men. Tom Jeffords and Cochise proved men from different races could become "blood brothers." Charles Goodnight opened the era of the cattle drives. Roy Rogers became a movie star and "King of the Cowboys." Johnny Appleseed not only planted fruit trees; he planted the seed of conservation and preservation. Chief Joseph lay down his rifle and told the white man, "From this day forward I shall fight no more forever."

Through bravery, courage and strength of character these men and women stood head and shoulders above their contemporaries. They are our true Western American Heroes.

ANNIE

Phoebe Ann Moses was born in a log cabin on the Ohio frontier. Her sisters called her Annie. When Annie was six her father died and Annie helped put food on the table by trapping and shooting small game animals.

She was sent away to live with another family, returning home when she was thirteen to find her mother still suffering financially and about to lose the family farm. Annie used her father's old Kentucky rifle to hunt game that she sold to hotels and restaurants in northern Ohio. She was such a prolific hunter that when she was fifteen she used her profits to retire the mortgage on the family farm.

Annie once paid $50 to enter a shooting contest against the famous marksman, Frank Butler. Frank laughed when he learned that a young woman would be his competition. In twenty-five shots Annie never missed. Frank missed once. Besides winning the contest, Annie won Frank Butler's heart and a year later they married. Annie went on tour with Frank and before long she was the star of the show and had adopted the stage name of Annie Oakley.

In 1885 Annie and Frank joined Buffalo Bill's Wild West Show and Annie became the featured attraction, displaying her amazingly accurate feats of shooting. A dime was tossed and Annie shot the coin in midair. Next a playing card was placed with the thin edge facing Annie, ninety feet away. Annie shot, flipped the card in the air, and punched a half-dozen more holes in the card before it hit the ground. She routinely shot a cigarette out of Frank's mouth and an apple off the head of their pet dog. One time she broke 4,472 out of 5,000 glass balls that were individually tossed in the air.

For twenty-one years Annie Oakley toured the world and then she abruptly retired from the public eye. Annie and Frank died in 1926, within three weeks of each other.

BUFFALO BILL

William F. Cody was born in Iowa Territory in 1846. When he was eight years old the family moved to Kansas. Indian boys from the nearby Kickapoo reservation became Will's playmates. His first horse was a Kickapoo pony.

At an early age Will learned to hunt and trap but he was forced to grow up quickly when his father died and Will, who was only eleven, became the family breadwinner. He continued to trap and hunt but he also recovered stolen horses for the Army at Ft. Leavenworth, drove freight wagons and rode for the Pony Express. At age eighteen he enlisted in the Union Army and served until the end of the Civil War.

Returning to Kansas Will signed on to supply buffalo meat to the crews building the Kansas-Pacific railroad. He was so successful at riding into a herd and shooting buffalo with his Springfield rifle that the railroad workers made up a song about him. The words to the tune included: "Buffalo Bill, Buffalo Bill/Never misses and never will/Always aims and shoots to kill/And the company pays his buffalo bill."

After that he was known far and wide as "Buffalo Bill" Cody. He served as a scout and guide for the Army during the Indian Wars and in 1872 he was awarded the Medal of Honor for his gallantry in a battle against a war party of Sioux in Nebraska. In 1883 he decided to assemble the stories and genuine people of the western frontier he had known over his lifetime and perform shows for eastern audiences. His Buffalo Bill's Wild West Show included a cast of up to six hundred Indians, cowboys and cowgirls, mountain men, and soldiers. There were wagons, stagecoaches, bucking broncs and stampeding buffalo. For thirty years the show, with Buffalo Bill as the star, toured North America and Europe. Buffalo Bill died in Denver, Colorado on January 10, 1917.

MARK TWAIN

Samuel Clemens was born in a small Missouri town. He said, "I increased the population by one per cent. It is more than many of the best men in history could have done for a town."

The family soon moved to Hannibal, Missouri where Samuel grew up. He left home at the age of eighteen, traveled to the east coast, returned to become a riverboat pilot on the Mississippi River and finally headed west to Virginia City, Nevada. He began writing humorous stories for the *Territorial Enterprise* newspaper under the pen name "Mark Twain," a term used on the Mississippi to indicate a depth of two fathoms.

After several years Samuel moved to San Francisco and worked as a reporter for the *Morning Call* newspaper and wrote for a number of magazines. A story titled, "The Celebrated Jumping Frog of Calaveras County," appeared in the New York *Saturday Press* and was republished across the nation. This propelled Samuel into the literary spotlight. He used his growing reputation to become an entertainer, appearing in theaters and regaling the audiences with humorous accounts of his adventures.

Samuel married in 1870, moved to Hartford, Connecticut and began his most productive years as a writer. *Tom Sawyer* was published in 1876, followed by the even more popular *Adventures of Huckleberry Finn*. In 1895 he made a grand world tour promoting his books and lectures. But the good times ended with the death of Samuel's wife. He wrote: "She was my life, and she is gone; she was my riches and I am a pauper." In the span of a few short years he also buried three of his four children. Samuel Clemens, one of the greatest figures of American literature, died of a broken heart on April 21, 1910.

DANIEL BOONE

Daniel Boone was born in 1734 in the Pennsylvania hill country. At an early age he began exploring the dense forest near his family's farm, making friends with the Indians and learning the habits of the wild animals.

After the outbreak of the French and Indian War Daniel joined a military expedition where he served with John Finley, a man who had explored the western regions and told fantastic tales of adventure. These stories ignited a passion in Daniel to see what lay over the next ridge.

Although Daniel returned home after the war and married a neighbor's daughter, Rebecca Bryan, he soon set off to explore the Kentucky hills. He spent the winter in a cabin and was joined by John Finley who persuaded Daniel to join a group of men traveling through the Cumberland Gap and on to the falls of the Ohio River. In his autobiography, published in 1784, Daniel tells of his many adventures: trailblazing a wilderness road through the Allegheny Mountains, founding a settlement he named Boonesborough on the Kentucky River, his capture at the hands of the Shawnee Indians, and his daring escape when he traveled 160 miles on foot in only four days.

Before the turn of the century Daniel claimed Kentucky had become too crowded for his liking. He and Rebecca moved to Missouri and although Daniel was an old man he made Missouri his base camp and continued to explore the land to the west. Rebecca died in 1813 and Daniel passed away seven years later. Their remains were moved from Missouri and re-interred in Kentucky in 1845. The memorial procession, led by a hearse drawn by four white horses, extended for more than a mile and was a fitting tribute to the man responsible, more than any other man, for the exploration and settlement of the state of Kentucky.

GERONIMO

The last major campaign of the western Indian wars was the Army's pursuit of the Apache warrior known as Geronimo. For nearly twenty years Geronimo outsmarted the troops, kept his band together and made a living raiding settlements in Mexico and across the border in what would become the state of Arizona.

Geronimo's Indian name was Goyathlay (One Who Yawns). He was peaceful until renegade Mexican soldiers attacked his camp while the men were away, stealing the horses and supplies and killing women and children. Geronimo's wife and three children were killed and he swore vengeance against the soldiers and vowed to fight the Mexicans and white settlers who were arriving and laying claim to the Apache homeland.

The final campaign against Geronimo and his followers was led by Brigadier General Nelson A. Miles and included a force of 5,000 troops and 500 Indian scouts. Over a five-month period they followed Geronimo more than 1,600 miles before General Miles, in a conference at Geronimo's camp on September 3, 1886, promised that if the Indians surrendered they would be exiled to Florida but allowed to return to Arizona.

The promise was broken. Geronimo and his fellow prisoners were shipped to Florida in a boxcar, imprisoned and forced to work at hard labor. Years passed and Geronimo was exiled to Oklahoma where he earned his living selling photographs of himself at fairs and on the street corner. Through it all he nourished a forlorn hope of seeing the deserts and rocky hills of his homeland one last time. It was not to be. He died February 17, 1909 and was buried at Fort Sill, Oklahoma.

BRONCHO BILLY

Max Aronson was a tall, gangly boy with a distinctive face. As a young man he moved from Arkansas to New York City to become a stage actor. He was turned down at every audition. Finally a theatrical agent suggested he go into the moving picture business.

At the time moving pictures were limited to one reel and ran about four minutes. Max came to the conclusion that if a story line were developed, customers would gladly sit still for an hour or more. For the first feature-length movie he suggested a western theme, with a thin plot padded with "lots of riding, shooting and plenty of excitement."

Max was hired as the star of the movie based on his claim to be a proficient rider and well-versed in handling a shooting iron. On the first day of filming he mounted his horse from the wrong side, the horse spooked and Max was promptly thrown. He was fired from the leading role but given several lesser parts. The movie, *The Great Train Robbery*, proved to be such a success that Max and a partner opened their own studio in Chicago and began cranking out westerns. They filmed up to five pictures a week with Max working as producer, director, studio head and star. He assumed the name "Broncho Billy" and between 1908 and 1915 nearly 400 westerns featuring the exploits of Broncho Billy were produced.

Within a few years of his retirement from the motion picture industry Max, trying to maintain an extravagant lifestyle, had frittered away his savings. He dropped out of sight and for years lived in obscurity. In 1958 he was presented with a special Academy Award recognizing him for creating the genre of cowboy westerns and acclaiming him as the world's first movie star. He died in 1971.

TOM HORN

Tom Horn ran away from home when he was fourteen. He worked on the railroad, freighted and drove stagecoach. By the time he was sixteen he was an army scout and involved in many Southwest Indian campaigns, including tracking down Geronimo.

After the Indian wars Horn became a gold miner and then a cowboy. In 1888 he entered the rodeo at Globe, Arizona and walked away with the title of World Champion steer roper. Two years later he joined the Pinkerton detective agency and was fearless in chasing down bank robbers and murderers. As a lawman it was claimed he killed seventeen men, all in the line of duty.

One day Horn stopped being a hero. He walked into the Pinkerton office and quit, saying, "I have no stomach for it anymore." When the Swan Land and Cattle Company came calling in 1894 Horn had the stomach to switch to the outlaw way of life. He was hired to methodically track down anyone he suspected of rustling and, using a high-powered buffalo rifle, ambush his man from long distance. As judge, jury and executioner Horn charged $600 for each rustler he dry-gulched.

Horn made a fatal mistake the morning of July 18, 1901. He lay in wait on a hill, planning to kill homesteader Kels Nickell, a man who had caused problems for the cattle barons of the region. When he saw a man come out of the cabin Horn pulled the trigger. The figure proved to be Kels's fourteen-year-old son Willie.

At his trial in Cheyenne, Horn was found guilty of murder. In the days before his execution Horn spent his time weaving the rope that would be used to hang him. On November 20, 1903 Tom Horn mounted the gallows. He told the executioner, "Hurry up, I got nothing more to say." And he was promptly hung.

PAUL KANE

Paul Kane was born in Ireland and immigrated to Canada with his family about 1822. At an early age Kane showed promise as an artist and was persuaded by a teacher to travel to Europe and learn from the master painters.

Not until Kane was thirty years old could he afford passage to Europe where he spent two years visiting art museums. During this time he made the decision to devote his life to painting, and determined his true calling was to record the cultures of the Indians of North America.

The Hudson's Bay Company had recently expanded its territory from the Great Lakes all the way to the Pacific Ocean and upon his return home Kane approached the company governor, George Simpson, and asked for his support. Simpson was skeptical and doubted whether Kane had the toughness and stamina necessary to travel with the fur brigades. Kane convinced him and in the end Simpson commissioned 100 paintings from Kane for which he agreed to pay $20,000.

On May 9, 1846 Kane departed for the Oregon Country. Over the course of the next seven months he traveled on steamships, canoes, horses and snowshoes to finally reach Fort Vancouver. That winter he sketched the Chinook and other tribes living along the lower Columbia River. In the spring he travel north to sketch the Indians around the Juan de Fuca Strait.

After spending a year among the Indians Kane returned to Toronto. An exhibit of 240 sketches from his trip met with such great success that Kane was heralded as a hero for having recorded the culture of the western Indians before it passed into oblivion. Kane died in 1871 but his work is still popular today. Collectors have paid more than $3 million for one of his paintings.

JOHN MARSHALL

John Marshall's great-grandfather was a signer of the Declaration of Independence and the family was well-established in New Jersey. But Marshall, seeking adventure, turned his back on the east coast and headed west.

He crossed the Oregon Trail in 1844 and found employment as a carpenter for John Sutter. He convinced Sutter of the need for a sawmill in the Sierra Nevada foothills and offered to go in partners with him. Marshall selected the location of the sawmill on the south fork of the American River, 45 miles northeast of Sutter's Fort.

Each night Marshall directed the river's flow through the millrace to carry away the debris that had gathered during the day. One morning, noticing a gold color at the bottom of the millrace, he scooped up several nuggets. He tested it by pounding the nuggets on an anvil and concluded it was soft and malleable just like gold. Next he tested the metal by boiling it with homemade soap and when it emerged untarnished he determined that indeed he had discovered gold.

Within a few months the area was overrun with miners. At first Marshall tried to charge a commission for any gold that was found. But the miners refused to pay. Marshall, possibly suffering a mental breakdown, claimed he heard voices that told him of the location of the mother lode. The miners refused to listen to him and drove him from one mining camp to the next. In his memoirs Marshall wrote: "I had to carry my pack of thirty or forty pounds over the mountains, living on China rice alone…. Thus I wandered for four years."

More than 20 years later the California State Legislature awarded Marshall a pension of $200 a month. By then he was 62 years old and in failing health. His pension was soon eliminated and he existed by selling autographed photographs of himself. He died in 1885.

GENTLEMAN JIM

For more than a decade John L. Sullivan held the world title as the bare-knuckle Heavyweight Champion. Fans were attracted to his marathon matches that lasted as many as seventy-five rounds. Because of the brutality many states and local jurisdictions outlawed bare-knuckle boxing and it became difficult for Sullivan to earn a living.

Jim Corbett began his boxing career at the time boxing was moving away from the bare-knuckle era to fighting with gloves. Jim represented the new age of boxing. He had attended college, worked as a bank clerk and had been trained by a professional coach. He dressed smartly and was well spoken. He became known as "Gentleman Jim."

On September 7, 1892 John L. Sullivan and Gentlemen Jim met in the first sanctioned World Heavyweight Championship title bout. This fight, held in New Orleans, attracted a crowd of over 10,000 fight fans and moved professional boxing out of the realm of criminal activity and into acceptable public entertainment.

Sullivan was the heavy favorite and won the first two rounds. Gentleman Jim did not throw a punch and the crowd began to hiss and demand that he stop running and start fighting. They were rewarded in the third round when Gentleman Jim came to life and broke Sullivan's nose. But not until the twenty-first round did the challenger hit the champion with a flurry of punches that caused Sullivan's eyes to roll back and his legs to buckle. He was not able to rise.

Gentleman Jim was crowned the world's first Heavyweight Champion under the Marquis of Queensberry rules. He held the title until losing to Bob Fitzsimmons in 1897. After that he became a stage actor and had a successful career in the movies.

JACK WILSON

His Indian name was Wovoka but the white settlers in Smith and Mason valleys of western Nevada knew him as Jack Wilson, the woodcutter. There was nothing noteworthy about the Indian until the day he had a sudden vision.

On January 1, 1889 Jack was cutting firewood in the Pine Grove Hills. That day there was a solar eclipse and Jack claimed that while the sun was hidden he was taken from this earth to heaven and spoke to his long dead ancestors and the Great Spirit who gave him instructions on how all Indians were to live. He immediately came down from the hills and began to preach, telling the Paiutes and Shoshones of his vision. His message was that all Indians were to abstain from fighting; they should work and learn from the white man and dance the traditional Round Dance. If they did these things they would be rewarded in the afterlife.

Not until Jack performed a series of miracles did he begin to develop a following. He predicted a rain that would end the long Nevada drought and clouds mysteriously appeared in the sky and rain began to fall. On a hot summer day he caused a river to freeze and to prove it was ice, he walked from one side to the other. In another display of his powers he directed rifles be fired at him and he deflected the bullets. Jack was hailed as a messenger of the Great Spirit and his new religion became known as the "Ghost Dance."

Jack told his grandson, "One day you shall fly in the sky like a hawk and be captain of men." The grandson grew up to become an Air Force captain and piloted a P-40 Warhawk with the Flying Tigers in World War II. Jack's last prediction was that when he died he would send an earthquake to signal his entrance into heaven. Jack died September 29, 1932 and three months later an earthquake rocked the Smith and Mason valleys.

JIM BOWIE

Jim Bowie was born in Kentucky in 1796. His father was a farmer and a slave owner and trader who frequently moved the family to the edge of the frontier. They lived in Tennessee, Missouri and Louisiana.

As a teenager Jim worked floating logs to a lumber mill. In his spare time he hunted and fished. He was described as rawboned and tough, with a quick, sometimes violent temper. He never backed away from a fight and carried a large hunting knife for protection.

During one particularly bloody fight, which became known as the Sandbar Fight, Jim exchanged shots with several men and finished off the affair by stabbing one of his assailants with his hunting knife. Witnesses remembered that distinctive knife and the prowess of the man wielding it. Blacksmiths were soon fashioning copies of the Bowie knife.

Jim drifted to Louisiana and began buying land. He acquired a sugar plantation of more than 1,800 acres and 80 slaves. But he felt tied down and sold his holdings. He traveled west into Texas, earning his living as a gambler.

When Mexico declared war on Texas, Jim was quick to side with the Texans. He was at the Alamo on March 6, 1836 when Mexican troops attacked before dawn and killed every last man. Jim Bowie will forever be remembered as a hero of Texas and the namesake of the famous Bowie knife.

DAVE MATHER

Dave Mather did not fit the image of a western hero. He was a frail-looking man with a quiet and reclusive air about him. The only hint at what he might become if provoked was in the outline of the twin Colt revolvers that bulged under his coat.

Mather was a frequent visitor to the saloons of Dodge City, Kansas. When he was not in a saloon Mather could usually be found sunning himself in a chair leaned against the wall of the marshal's office. Oftentimes Marshal Tom Carson sat with Mather, quietly watching the street and the comings and goings of citizens and visitors.

One evening Marshal Carson was jumped by a group of men known as the Henry gang. They drew on the marshal, fired a volley of shots and the marshal fell to the floor mortally wounded. Mather rushed to his side and before the lawman died he promised to settle the score, vowing, "I'll kill every last one of them."

Mather ran from the room and dashed down the street. With both guns drawn he called to the Henry gang to stop and surrender. The desperadoes went for their weapons and Mather systematically gunned them down in a spectacular blaze of gunfire. When it was over seven men were left dead or dying.

After the shootout Mather thought he could remain the anonymous gunslinger he had always been, but he was involved in another shootout and was forced to kill his opponent. He soon realized that as long as he remained in Dodge City others would come to test his reputation. One day Mather saddled his horse and left town. He arrived in San Francisco, took passage on a ship bound for Canada and enlisted in the Royal Canadian Mounted Police. He never returned to the States to claim his position as one of the great gunfighters of the Old West.

JEREMIAH JOHNSON

The fact and fiction of the life of Jeremiah Johnson is blurred. Historians agree that Johnson was a large man, standing six feet tall and weighing a solid 200 pounds. It is believed he was born in New Jersey and that he came west during the Mexican American War. After the fighting ended he traveled north, became a hunter and trapper and lived among the Indians. He took an Indian wife.

In 1847 a party of Crow warriors killed his wife and Johnson swore revenge against the entire Crow nation. He carried out his personal war, hunting down and killing Crow warriors at every opportunity. According to the legend, Johnson always scalped his victims and gained his revenge by eating the dead man's liver, giving rise to his nickname, "Liver-eating Johnson."

After a quarter-century of killing, Johnson declared his personal vendetta against the Crow had been satisfied. He left the frontier. During the Civil War he joined the Union forces and served as a sharpshooter with Company H, Second Colorado Cavalry. Later he was appointed deputy sheriff in Leadville, Colorado and was the town marshal in Red Lodge, Montana. He died in Los Angeles on January 21, 1900 and was buried there.

The story of Liver-Eating Johnson remained an obscure western legend until the movie *Jeremiah Johnson* was released in 1972. The movie, never hinting at Johnson's cannibalism, starred Robert Redford as Jeremiah Johnson. Within two years of the movie's release the body of the man who had become an overnight hero was removed from its resting place in the Los Angeles cemetery and reburied in Cody, Wyoming. Robert Redford served as one of the pallbearers.

SOAPY SMITH

Jefferson Randolph Smith was born in 1860 to a wealthy Georgia plantation owner but he left home to become a cowpuncher. At the end of his first trail drive he bumped into the gamblers and con men and was fascinated by their ability to separate the cowboys from their hard-earned cash. He quickly determined the gambler's lifestyle suited him better than trailing a bunch of cattle down a dusty trail.

Smith was a fast learner and soon became proficient at slight of hand tricks. His sport of choice was an adaptation of the old shell game. He played the game by setting up a folding table along a busy street. As a crowd began to gather he entertained them with humorous stories and light banter while twisting paper around ordinary bars of soap. He made a spectacle of placing a ten, twenty or even $100 bill inside some of these packages. To start the action Smith had a shill step forward, pay five dollars, take a bar of soap and discover he was the lucky winner of one hundred dollars. But many of the customers ended up with nothing more than a nickel bar of soap. Smith was so good at the game he became know as "Soapy" Smith.

The nature of his livelihood required Soapy to be constantly on the move. He made his way to Creede, Colorado, where the silver mines were producing $1 million a month, and quickly amassed a fortune. But Soapy turned right around and spent the money to benefit the town, putting up cash to build a new church, supporting widows or families down on their luck, grubstaking miners, and even helping some of the sporting girls turn their lives around.

After becoming a local hero Soapy moved on to Skagway, Alaska where his high-flying life ended tragically in a barroom gunfight. At the time of his death he was thirty-eight years old and his entire estate totaled a measly $250.

DEAD MAN'S HAND

Wild Bill Hickok was tall, lean and ruggedly handsome. He typically had a lawman's badge pinned to his vest and it was said he was so quick with the twin revolvers he carried tucked in his belt that he could draw and shoot faster than the human eye could blink.

James Butler "Wild Bill" Hickok was born in Troy Grove, Illinois in 1837. When the Civil War broke out he became a civilian scout for the Union forces at Fort Leavenworth, Kansas. After the war he drifted to Springfield, Missouri where he got into a fight over the favor of a woman with a former Confederate soldier named David Tutt. They settled their differences in the street, drawing six-guns and firing at each other in what has been recognized as the first classic Wild West shoot-out. Wild Bill won the contest. David Tutt lost his life.

Wild Bill's reputation was embellished by newspaper reports and dime novels that related a wide array of his exploits. He also traveled with his good friend Buffalo Bill Cody where he played himself in the "Scouts of the Plains." But he soon tired of the constant travel and returned to the West where he became the town marshal of Abilene, Kansas. Oftentimes a rowdy cowhand would think twice about disturbing the peace if he knew he had to face Wild Bill Hickok. But fame proved to be a double-edged sword.

On the afternoon of August 2, 1876 Wild Bill was playing poker in Saloon #10 in Deadwood, Dakota Territory. Jack McCall, who blamed Wild Bill for the death of his brother, sneaked up from behind and shot Wild Bill in the back of the head. At the time of his death Wild Bill was holding a hand with a pair of aces and a pair of eights. Those cards became known as the "dead man's hand."

HOOT

Ed Gibson grew up on a farm and cattle ranch in Nebraska but the only thing that ever interested him were horses. He was horse crazy.

The family moved to Los Angeles and Ed was forced to give up his horses. To keep himself busy he took a part-time job delivering medicine for the Owl Drug Company. According to Ed, "When my classmates found out they gave me the nickname 'Hoot Owl,' then it got shortened to 'Hoot' and that name just sort of stuck."

Even though Hoot was trapped in the city he practiced his roping skills and found a way to be around horses. After school he rode horses for a western show based in Los Angeles and wrangled for the motion picture industry.

In 1912 Hoot visited the Pendleton Round-Up where he won the All-Around Cowboy title. He swung north to Calgary and added the distinction of becoming the World Champion Fancy Roper at the Calgary Stampede. For several years he traveled to rodeos in the summer and spent winters in Hollywood, working as a double to some of the biggest western motion picture stars and performing such dangerous stunts as leaping from the back of a galloping horse onto a moving train.

Hoot interrupted his movie career to enlist in the tank corps during World War I. When he returned in 1919 he signed with Universal and made the transition to talking movies, drawing a salary of $14,000 a week. He spent the money just as fast on cars, airplanes and leading ladies.

Over his lifetime Hoot made a fortune but he blew it all on his lavish lifestyle, bad investments and a succession of wives. The last few years of his life he was reduced to acting as a greeter at the Last Frontier casino in Las Vegas. He died broke in 1962.

PAT GARRETT

Pat Garrett was a tall, skinny kid who quit school early, gathered up his squirrel rifle and little else, and headed from his family home in Louisiana. In New Mexico he caught on as a horse wrangler for rancher Pete Maxwell.

Working for the same outfit was a young buck-toothed fellow named William Bonney. The two became best friends, working and playing together, traveling to attend fandangos and card games and spending wild nights at local drinking establishments. But within a few years the two men had taken different paths in life. William Bonney became known as Billy the Kid, an outlaw and gunfighter. Pat Garrett became a lawman.

In his autobiography Garrett recalled that he caught up with Billy the Kid at Pete Maxwell's ranch on July 14, 1881. It was near midnight and Garrett had gone to Pete's bedroom to ask him of the Kid's whereabouts. While they were quietly conversing, the front door opened and Billy the Kid stepped inside. Garrett wrote, "From his step I could perceive he was either barefooted or in his stocking-feet. The Kid must have seen, or felt, my presence at the head of the bed. He raised quickly his pistol, a self-cocker, within a foot of my breast. I drew my revolver and fired, threw my body aside, and fired again. The second shot was useless; the Kid fell dead. He never spoke."

Pat Garrett collected the $500 reward but the general feeling of the community was that Billy the Kid should have been gunned down in a fair fight, not in the middle of the night and in his stocking feet. After that Pat Garrett was considered more of a villain than a true hero and few tears were shed when, in 1908, a man slipped up behind Pat Garrett and fired a bullet into the back of his head, killing him instantly.

WEST OF THE PECOS

The colorful life of Judge Roy Bean has been the subject of books, movies and even a television series. His notoriety made him a hero to some, but during his life he was never considered a heroic figure.

Roy Bean was born in Kentucky about 1825. He left home at age 15, traveled west and landed in California. After shooting a man in a duel he moved to New Mexico and drifted on into Texas. It was said that Roy never made an honest dollar. He was a thief, smuggler and a swindler. He arrived in West Texas in 1882 and set up a saloon in a tent beside the railroad being built between San Antonio and El Paso. A tent town sprang up around his saloon and Roy bragged he named the town Langtry, after the beautiful British actress, Lilly Langtry. He went so far as to hang a picture of Miss Lilly behind the bar and wrote many letters to her inviting her to come west and visit the town he had named in her honor.

Roy pulled a few strings and had himself named Justice of the Peace of Precinct No. 6 in Pecos County. He operated his court from his saloon, posting signs out front proclaiming "ICE COLD BEER" and "LAW WEST OF THE PECOS." It was said he began each trial by muttering, "We ought to hang 'em first an' try 'em later."

Most of Roy's criminal cases consisted of misdemeanor counts of drunkenness and petty larceny, two crimes with which Roy was well acquainted. He allowed a minimum of testimony, made his ruling quickly and pocketed the fines he imposed.

In March 1903, Roy went on a drinking binge and died. A short time later Miss Lilly, on her way from New Orleans to San Francisco, stopped at her namesake town. In her autobiography she noted, "It was a short visit, but an unforgettable one."

CRAZY HORSE

Crazy Horse, a Lakota Sioux, was born about 1849. As a boy he had a vision of a mighty storm and a rider on horseback. This man had long, unbraided hair, a small stone in his ear and was wearing decorative paint depicting zigzagging lightning bolts on his face and round marks like rain dotting his body. People ran to him and though they tried to touch him he was like a ghost.

"You have seen a very powerful vision," said Crazy Horse's father, a medicine man. "You will be a great warrior and a leader of men."

By the time Crazy Horse was twelve years old he had already killed his first buffalo. When he was thirteen he stole horses from a Crow camp. And by twenty he was leading a war party. He waged war against the miners who traveled the Bozeman Trail to the goldfields of Montana and helped to defeat the American soldiers at Fort Phil Kearny. At every opportunity Crazy Horse fought to prevent encroachment on Lakota lands. When the government ordered all Lakota onto reservations Crazy Horse became a leader of the resistance, joining forces with Sitting Bull and destroying Custer's Seventh Cavalry at the battle of Little Bighorn.

After the battle many of the participants fled to Canada, but Crazy Horse and his followers remained and carried on a running fight against the forces of General Nelson Miles. Word was sent to Crazy Horse that if he quit fighting his followers would receive a reservation in the Powder River country. Crazy Horse refused but eventually, his people weary from the constant military harassment and starving because there were no buffalo, he led 800 followers to Fort Robinson and surrendered. Four months later, while in custody, Crazy Horse was bayoneted in the abdomen by a soldier. He died September 5, 1877.

BAT MASTERSON

William Barclay "Bat" Masterson was born in Quebec, Canada in 1853. The Masterson family soon moved to a farm in Illinois.

At age seventeen Bat left home seeking adventure. In Kansas he joined a buffalo-hunting outfit. After that he drifted around taking odd jobs and finally landed in the Texas Panhandle town of Mobeetie where a man took offense to the amount of time Bat was spending with a particular saloon girl. In the ensuing gunfight Bat killed the man but took a bullet in his hip that caused him to limp for the remainder of his life. Bat never allowed the injury to slow him and in the next few years he enhanced his reputation as a gunfighter by working in law enforcement alongside such men as Wyatt Earp, Doc Holiday and Charlie Bassett. When Bat did not have a star pinned on his chest he drank in the saloons and made his living gambling and promoting horse races.

One day Bat wrote a story about one of his escapades. It was published in a local newspaper. Everyone liked the story and this encouraged Bat to spend less time drinking and gambling and more time writing. He was hired by the New York *Morning Telegraph* newspaper, moved back to the East Coast and became such a popular writer that in 1905, when President Teddy Roosevelt tried to hire him as a U.S. Marshal, Bat turned him down, telling the president, "I have taken my guns off, and I don't ever want to put them on again."

The morning of October 25, 1921 Bat sat at his desk and wrote: "There are those who argue that everything breaks even ... that because the rich man gets ice in the summer and the poor man gets it in the winter things are breaking even for both. Maybe so, but I'll swear I can't see it that way." Those were the last words of Bat Masterson. He was found slumped over his desk. He died of a heart attack.

CHIEF JOSEPH

Old Chief Joseph, the leader of the Wallowa band of the Nez Perce, was friendly to the white man, but when promises were not kept he soon became suspicious. On his deathbed he told his son, Young Chief Joseph, "This country holds your father's body. Never sell the bones of your father."

Young Chief Joseph took his father's words to heart. He tried to live in peace but conflicts became unavoidable. Gold was discovered on Nez Perce land. Following in the miners' footsteps came pioneers who laid claim to the best grazing land. In response to this onslaught the federal government summarily reduced the Nez Perce reservation from 5,000 square miles to roughly 500 square miles. In 1877 the Wallowa Valley was declared to be government land and Chief Joseph and his followers were given thirty days to leave or be forcibly removed.

The Nez Perce began to round up their horses but a number of the young warriors revolted and went on a killing spree, forcing the Nez Perce to retreat before the Army could retaliate. Over the next four months an estimated 1,000 Nez Perce, the majority of them women and children, carried on a running battle with the Army as they traveled 1,700 miles across the mountains before being forced to surrender at Bear Paw, barely forty miles from safe haven in Canada. As Chief Joseph laid down his rifle he said, "From this day forward I shall fight no more forever."

The Nez Perce were taken into custody as prisoners of war and exiled to the Oklahoma Indian Territory. After eight years many were relocated to the Colville Indian Reservation near Nespelem, Washington. Although a promise had been made that Young Chief Joseph would be returned to his homeland in the Wallowa Valley that promise was never kept. He died September 21, 1904.

THE PATHFINDER

John Charles Fremont was born out of wedlock in 1813. He worked hard in school, joined the Army Corps of Topographical Engineers and dreamed of traveling to the far West and somehow making a name for himself. At the age of 26 he met Senator Thomas Hart Benton who invited him home for dinner. Fremont was introduced to the Senator's strong-willed 15-year-old daughter Jessie and two years later they married.

Soon the Senator, the powerful chairman of the Senate Committee on Military Affairs, gave his son-in-law command of an expedition to the Rocky Mountains. Fremont used the command to further his career by writing a book about the journey that became a best seller. He parlayed his fame into securing command of a second exploration to the West. This journey took him from the Great Salt Lake to the Northwest and then to California and into the Southwest before returning to St. Louis. It was the most ambitious government-sponsored expedition since Lewis and Clark traveled to the Pacific.

Fremont once again wrote of his wanderings and the early pioneers used his descriptions and detailed maps to guide them to Oregon and California. Fremont was heralded as the "Great Pathfinder" but he turned his back on fame and civilization and undertook a third expedition. He arrived in California and, seeing war with Mexico was inevitable, he used his men as an invading army and forced the nominal commander of northern California to surrender. Fremont assumed control of California but when the U. S. Army arrived, Fremont was unceremoniously relieved of his position.

Fremont returned to his wife and launched an unsuccessful bid for the presidency. He was appointed as governor of the Arizona territory and died in 1890.

SWEET MEDICINE

The Cheyenne dwelled in permanent villages and farmed the riverbanks growing corn, squash and beans in what is now the state of Minnesota. Their warring neighbors, the Lakota, drove the Cheyenne from their homeland and forced them to settle in what is now South Dakota. Here they hunted buffalo on foot and continued to farm.

One night Sweet Medicine, a Cheyenne prophet, had a powerful dream. He told his people that a strange animal would appear and forever change the Cheyenne way of life. He claimed this four-footed animal would be a beast of burden and would have round hooves, a shaggy mane, and a tail that would touch the ground.

Many years passed and Sweet Medicine died. During this time the Spaniards, in search of the fabled Seven Cities of Gold, introduced the horse to North America. A few horses escaped, or were stolen and traded, and by the 1700s horses began to appear on the Plains. According to legend the first horse to arrive in the land of the Cheyenne was seen drinking from a lake. The prophecy of Sweet Medicine was immediately recalled and a celebration was held in his honor.

Near the lake a snare was set and when the horse returned for water he stepped into the snare. Warriors rushed to him and tied him down before he could injure himself. The Cheyenne broke this horse to ride and pack. And when they learned there were more horses to the south they went there and traded for them.

The horse changed the Cheyenne way of life. They soon abandoned their fields and permanent villages and became nomadic hunters, following the herds of buffalo and raiding other tribes to add ponies to their herds. The vision of Sweet Medicine had come to pass.

JOE WALKER

Joseph Rutherford Walker was born to wander the far reaches of the western frontier. He grew up hunting and trapping and his first adventure away from home began when he was fifteen years old. He joined a company of mounted riflemen and fought under Andrew Jackson in the Indian Wars of 1812-1815.

After the fighting ended Walker drifted westward and when a survey crew was organized to establish the route of the Santa Fe Trail, young Joe Walker was hired as a scout and hunter for the party. In 1830 he met Captain Benjamin Bonneville who was leaving for an ambitious trapping expedition to the Rocky Mountains and beyond. Walker was hired as chief guide of the expedition and successfully led the large delegation of trappers to California. It was here that Governor Jose Figueroa took a liking to Walker and offered him seven square miles of land. But Walker was not ready to settle down and abruptly left California. For the next decade he roamed the country, trapping, hunting and trading horses among the Indian tribes.

Gold was discovered in California and Walker began guiding miners to the diggings as well as engaging in a freighting business, bringing supplies to the settlements in the foothills of the Sierra Nevada. With the area becoming too populated for Walker's liking he set off once again, exploring the canyons of what would one day become the states of Utah and Arizona. In his travels he discovered petrified forests and ruins of lost civilizations.

In 1867 Walker retired from his wandering ways and settled on his nephew's ranch near Walnut Creek, California. He lived out his days here and was buried on a rise overlooking the confluence of the Sacramento and San Joaquin rivers.

DEADWOOD DICK

Nat Love was born a slave in the hill country of Tennessee. Shortly after the Civil War fifteen-year-old Nat decided to spread his wings and experience freedom.

It was his dream to become a cowboy. He gathered his few belongings and headed west, landing in the frontier town of Dodge City, Kansas where he signed on to work as a cowboy for a dollar a day. Nat was a natural cowboy and a quick learner who never shied away from hard work, just as long as a horse and a cow were involved.

One day Nat asked the trail boss of a Texas outfit for a job and the boss agreed, on the condition that Nat could ride Good Eye, the rankest horse in the remuda. Nat rode the horse to a standstill and was hired on the spot. He worked in the Texas Panhandle, the Gila River country of Arizona and throughout the Southwest.

In the spring of 1876 Nat was on a drive that brought 3,000 head of steers to Deadwood City in the Dakota Territory. They arrived in time for the town's big Fourth of July celebration. The highlight of the day was a cowboy contest. Nat entered and took his turn in the wild horse competition, roping, throwing, saddling and riding his mustang in nine minutes flat. In the shooting events Nat hit the bull's eye fourteen times in a row. The town presented Nat with $200 in prize money, proclaimed him the best cowboy in the world and gave him a nickname, "Deadwood Dick."

In 1890 Nat retired from the life of a cowboy. He took one of the few jobs available to a black man, on the railroad as a Pullman porter. He died at the age of fifty-three in 1907.

BANDIT QUEEN

Pearl Taylor became a western heroine for all the wrong reasons. She was born into a well-to-do family in Ontario, Canada and attended private schools. Then she fell in love with Fredrick Hart, a gambler and a ladies' man, and her structured world quickly unraveled.

Hart and Pearl married and honeymooned at the Columbian Exposition of 1893 in Chicago where Pearl was introduced to the American West as portrayed in the Wild West shows. She abruptly left her husband and traveled west.

In 1899 Pearl received a letter stating her family had fallen on hard times and her mother was ill and needed money to pay her medical bills. Pearl confided her predicament to a friend, Joe Boot, and he devised a plan to rob the Globe stagecoach. With guns drawn Pearl and Joe stopped the stage. Pearl ushered the passengers out of the coach and forced them to empty their pockets, wallets and purses. She collected about $450.

When they tried to escape Pearl and Joe became hopelessly lost and were soon overtaken by a posse. Pearl Hart played up her part as a heroine, having taken the money to help her sick mother. Large crowds gathered at the Globe jail for a glimpse of the woman the newspapers called the "Bandit Queen."

At her trial the jury acquitted her but the judge ordered her retried. This time Pearl was found guilty and was sentenced to five years in prison. After serving eighteen months she was released and profited from her fame by touring the country and starring in a play titled "Lady Bandit." But the tour ended abruptly and Pearl dropped from the public eye. No one is sure what happened to the unlikely heroine but it is claimed she lived a quiet life in San Francisco and died in 1952.

YAKIMA CANUTT

His name was Enos Edward Canutt but he became famous to a legion of fans around the world as Yakima, or just plain Yak. Born in Colfax, Washington, Yakima became active in rodeos and wild west shows while he was a teenager. He acquired his nickname from a rodeo announcer who erroneously introduced him as the Cowboy from Yakima. He went on to become a World Saddlebronc Champion and won the All-Around Cowboy title at the Pendleton Round-Up.

His success as a rodeo performer led Yakima to Hollywood where he became a stuntman and actor in a string of silent movies. He is credited with the development of the screen brawl where actors fight in a choreographed battle and, because of the positioning of the camera, it appears they are landing punches, while in reality their fists never make contact.

In *Cyclone of the Saddle* he secured knife blades to the ends of a pair of bullwhips and used these to kill his adversaries. He doubled Clark Gable and drove the buckboard while Atlanta burned in *Gone With the Wind*. During the Indian attack in John Ford's *Stagecoach* he leaped from his horse onto a six-horse team, was shot and fell underneath the fast moving team and the stagecoach passed over him. He performed the same stunt in *Zorro's Fighting Legion*. And he staged the memorable action scenes in the chariot race segments in the 1959 film *Ben-Hur*.

It is estimated that Yakima appeared in over 1,000 films. He was given a star on the Hollywood Walk of Fame, was inducted into the National Cowboy & Western Heritage Hall of Fame, and in 1966 was presented a special Academy Award for a lifetime as a premier stunt developer and performer. He died in 1986 at the age of 89 in North Hollywood, California.

DAVY CROCKETT

Davy Crockett was born in 1786 near the mouth of Limestone Creek in what would become the state of Tennessee. He was the fifth of nine children and split his time playing in the outdoors and passing time in the log cabin tavern operated by his father. Davy listened to the stories the travelers told about the wilderness to the west and it sparked his desire for a life of adventure.

When Davy was thirteen his father sent him to school but after only four days Davy got in a fight and, rather than face a whipping from his father, he ran away from home. He found employment driving a herd of cattle to Virginia and stayed on there working for farmers, freighters and a hat maker. After two years he returned home.

Davy went to work for one of the neighbors and in his spare time he practiced shooting his rifle and developing his hunting skills. He became so proficient he won most of the local shooting contests, paying two bits for a single shot at a target, the one closest to the bulls-eye winning a quarter of beef. Davy's aim was so true he often took home the entire beef.

Once again Davy returned to school, this time his studies lasted six months before he abruptly quit to go to work and get married. He fought in the Creek Indian War, became a representative to the Tennessee legislature, and was elected to Congress where he became famous for his backwoods stories and humorous speeches.

In 1835 Davy led a group of Tennessee volunteers to Texas to fight in the war against Mexico. It was at the Alamo in March 1836 that Davy Crockett, along with a force of 186 men, refused to surrender to the 4,000 troops in the Mexican army. The Americans fought to the last man in the Battle of the Alamo.

BUFFALO JONES

Charles Jesse Jones was born in Illinois in 1844. He came west in his early twenties and became a cowboy and a legendary buffalo hunter. He killed so many buffalo that he was given the nickname Buffalo Jones.

Jones married and settled on a homestead that would one day become Garden City, Kansas. He soon realized that the buffalo were fast disappearing from the Plains and made many adventure-filled trips to capture buffalo cows and calves and bring them to his homestead. During the devastating winter of 1886 thousands of range cattle perished on the Plains but the buffalo seemed immune to the cold and continued to forage for food. It occurred to Jones that he should crossbreed cattle with his buffalo. He called the offspring "cattalo" and actively promoted his new breed. Ultimately the experiment failed when the cattalo failed to breed.

Jones amassed the largest private herd of buffalo in Kansas, close to 150 head, but during the financial turmoil of the 1890s he was forced to sell his herd to pay his mounting debts. Theodore Roosevelt appointed Buffalo Jones as the first game warden of Yellowstone National Park and in 1906 he established a buffalo game preserve on the north rim of the Grand Canyon. Three years later he traveled to Africa where he lassoed, captured and photographed a large assortment of wild animals.

A book about his exploits, *Roping Lions in Africa*, brought Jones wide acclaim and recognition. Zane Grey wrote several books about Jones's exploits, including *Last of the Plainsmen*. And Edward VII, King of England, awarded him a medal of honor for his work with animals. Charles Jesse Jones died in 1919. He will be remembered not as Buffalo Jones, the buffalo killer, but for his work in helping to save the American Bison from extinction.

BIDWELL

John Bidwell was a twenty-one-year-old schoolteacher when a French-Canadian trader told him of the wonders of a region called California. Bidwell immediately organized a company of 68 men who shared his dream of moving west and starting a new life in California.

"We were ready to start," Bidwell said, "but no one knew the way. All we knew was that California lay to the west, and that was the extent of our knowledge."

Mountain man Thomas Fitzpatrick came to their rescue and, since he was already employed to guide a party to Oregon, he offered to lead Bidwell to the parting of the ways where the trail to California swung south. When they reached the parting of the ways nearly half of Bidwell's party, frightened at venturing into unknown territory without a guide, continued on with Fitzpatrick.

Bidwell and thirty-one companions were soon forced to abandon their wagons. They slaughtered the oxen for food and as they continued toward the towering Sierras they were forced to eat crows, coyotes and even insects. They fought their way over the mountains to the San Joaquin Valley.

Bidwell found employment with John Sutter, the most important foreigner in California and a man who controlled nearly 50,000 acres at the confluence of the Sacramento and American rivers. The following year 125 Americans followed Bidwell's footsteps to California and in 1845 the emigrants numbered over 3,000. And at Bidwell's urging Sutter provided the newcomers with the supplies and shelter they needed.

HOLLYWOOD COWBOY

Tom Mix was a man of contradictions. He was born in the East but became the biggest cowboy star of the silent film era. The fans who packed the theaters knew the name Tom Mix meant adventure, excitement, and hard-riding action.

It is difficult to separate the real Tom Mix from the Hollywood hype. According to publicity generated by studios Mix rode with Teddy Roosevelt as he led the charge of San Juan Hill in the Spanish American War, served with honor as a Texas Ranger and was a mercenary in the Boxer Rebellion in China. The actual facts show he served an uneventful stint in the U.S. Army and the closest he came to the Texas Rangers was in 1935 when the governor of Texas made him an Honorary Ranger.

Mix, born in Pennsylvania in 1880, appeared in his first silent film in 1909. Most of his early works were "shorts", with one or two reels. As Mix's popularity grew, the length of his films expanded to five or six reels. During his storied career he made more than 300 films. What set him apart from other actors were his rugged good looks and his convincing portrayal of a western cowboy. He was a skilled rider and performed his own tricks and stunts, even the most dangerous. He played characters who had a positive influence on his young viewers, wore flashing western garb and a big cowboy hat. He was a showman and his salary of $17,000 a week, the largest in the film industry at the time, proved his worth as a performer.

Mix wore fancy clothes, rode expensive horses and drove around in classy automobiles. He attended lavish parties, wined and dined starlets and leading ladies and was married five times. Tom Mix died on a lonely stretch of highway in the Arizona desert. He was driving his 1937 Cord Phaeton convertible fast, lost control and ran off the road. The Hollywood cowboy, the legend, was dead.

CYNTHIA ANN PARKER

Comanche raiders kidnapped nine-year-old Cynthia Ann Parker from her parents' Texas home. The young girl quickly adjusted to the Indian life and as a teenager she became the wife of Peta Nocona, a rising young chief. She bore him three children, two sons and a daughter — Quanah, Pecos and Prairie Flower. Even though most men took several wives Peta was pleased with Cynthia Ann and remained monogamous to her.

Content to live with the Comanche, Cynthia Ann claimed she had no desire to ever rejoin the civilized world, not even when white buffalo hunters met her on the Plains and proposed to pay a ransom for her freedom. She refused their offer and, speaking the Comanche language and making sign, she made it clear she wished to be left alone, saying she had children to care for and a husband she loved.

In December 1860 a group of Texas Rangers and U.S. cavalrymen attacked the Comanche village and took the woman with Caucasian features and blue eyes as their captive. The woman spoke only Comanche but it was suspected she was Cynthia Ann Parker, the white woman known to be living among the Comanches for the past 24 years.

Isaac Parker, Cynthia Ann's uncle, positively identified her as his niece. He took her and her daughter Prairie Flower back to east Texas to live with the Parker clan. All during the time Cynthia Ann lived with her natural family she repeatedly tried to escape and return to the Comanche village. Each time well-meaning relatives brought her back. Then in 1864 Prairie Flower died. Cynthia Ann, overcome with grief and longing for her adopted people, starved herself to death.

CHIEF SEATTLE

Chief Seattle was born about 1786 on an island in Puget Sound. As a child he witnessed the arrival of sailing ships and white men who traded trinkets, cloth, iron, guns and alcohol in exchange for valuable furs.

In later years Chief Seattle welcomed the white settlers who had crossed the Oregon Trail by covered wagons and streamed into the Puget Sound area in the 1840s. As a show of his good intentions Chief Seattle vowed to cease making war against neighboring tribes, was baptized into the white man's religion, released his slaves, and was the first to sign a treaty relinquishing land to the new arrivals.

In appreciation the Americans named their growing settlement in honor of Chief Seattle. But within a few years an ordinance was enacted in the newly incorporated town forbidding Indians to live within the city limits. Chief Seattle was forced to move but he remained a common sight, wandering around town until his death in 1866.

Chief Seattle became more famous in death than in life. A speech attributed to Chief Seattle appeared in an environmental film documentary that was aired on national television in 1971. The speech was subsequently read at Earth Day celebrations. The words, eloquent and moving, extolled the virtues of the Indian way of living in harmony with nature and assailed the white man for polluting the world and destroying nature. Chief Seattle became an icon of the "green" movement and was proclaimed an early day environmental prophet.

But Chief Seattle never spoke the words. Ted Perry, an East Coast scriptwriter and college professor, wrote the prose attributed to Chief Seattle. Yet the myth persists. There have been films, posters and even a best-selling book based on the speech. Chief Seattle has become a modern day folk hero.

KING OF THE COWBOYS

Leonard Franklin Slye was born in 1911. His father was an Ohio farmer and his mother was part Choctaw Indian. They taught their son to ride horses, sing, play the guitar and instilled in him a strong sense of right and wrong.

After the stock market crashed in 1929 Leonard joined a caravan of Dust Bowl migrants headed toward California. He arrived with little more than a change of clothes and his guitar slung over his shoulder. He picked fruit, drove truck and played music and sang at every opportunity.

In 1936 Leonard married Arlene Wilkins. He found it difficult to support a wife and when he happened to see an advertisement seeking a singing cowboy for an upcoming movie he sneaked into a casting call and was immediately offered a contract at Republic Pictures for $75 a week. When it came time to list Leonard in the credits the movie executives wanted to name their new actor Dick Weston, but at the last minute decided on Roy Rogers.

Over the next sixty years Roy Rogers recorded 400 songs and starred in more than 100 movies. In all his films he played the role of the western hero, always standing for justice in the end. He was kind to animals, God-fearing, humble and a role model to legions of young fans, counseling them to always "Be neat and clean" and "Study hard and learn all you can." His name and likeness was plastered on everything from school lunch pails and cap pistols to more than two billion boxes of Post breakfast cereal.

Roy's wife died and in 1946 he married Dale Evans, his co-star in the movies. They established a museum, now located in Branson, Missouri, that preserves memorabilia from their lives, including the mounted remains of their horses Trigger and Buttermilk and their faithful dog Bullet. Roy Rogers, the "King of the Cowboys," died in 1998.

HANGING JUDGE

After the Civil War the Oklahoma Indian Territory was a lawless frontier, populated by Indians displaced from their native lands and bands of roving outlaws. The desperados were of the opinion that the law could not touch them as long as they remained in Indian Territory. But all that changed with the arrival of Judge Isaac Parker.

Isaac Charles Parker was born in a log cabin in Ohio, attended law school and was admitted to the Ohio bar when he was only twenty-one years old. He built a solid reputation as an honest lawyer and was elected to Congress. When his political career ended he was appointed federal judge in the western district of Arkansas, an area that included the Oklahoma Indian Territory.

Judge Parker vowed to bring law and order to the region. A week after assuming his post, eighteen men charged with murder were brought before him and he found fifteen guilty and sentenced eight to die on the gallows. Before the sentence could be carried out one man was killed trying to escape and another, because of his young age, had his sentence commuted to life in prison.

The hanging of the remaining six men took place September 3, 1875 and was an extraordinary public spectacle. More than 5,000 persons witnessed the condemned men die on the gallows and many of the Eastern newspapers sent reporters and photographers to cover the event. The newspapers proclaimed Judge Parker the "Hanging Judge."

During the twenty-one years he sat on the bench Judge Parker sentenced 168 men and four women to hang. The irony was that Judge Parker actually favored the abolition of the death penalty. He died in 1896; six weeks after federal authorities closed his court.

NARCISSA

Narcissa Prentiss was born in 1808 in the state of New York. At a very young age she had a religious awakening and made the decision to dedicate her life to missionary work among the native people of the American Far West.

After completing her education and teaching school for several years, Narcissa applied to the American Board of the Congregational Church for missionary work. Her request was denied because the Board was unwilling to send unmarried women as missionaries. But Narcissa soon met Marcus Whitman, a man who had offered himself for missionary work, and they agreed to marry and travel west together. The Board immediately offered them positions as missionaries in the Oregon country.

The day following the wedding Narcissa said goodbye to her family and friends. She would never see them again. But through the letters she sent to them, letters that were published in the East, Narcissa became one of the most famous personalities of the missionary era.

The Whitmans established their mission among the Cayuse Indians in the Walla Walla Valley and Narcissa, who had become pregnant on the journey west, gave birth the following spring to a daughter, Alice Clarissa. At first the letters Narcissa sent home were happy and optimistic but when Alice drowned in the Walla Walla River, Narcissa became depressed.

Work at the mission failed because the Cayuse refused to adopt the white man's religion and were suspicious and felt threatened by the missionaries and the horde of wagon emigrants who were streaming into the country. On November 29, 1947 the Indians attacked the mission, burned the buildings to the ground and murdered fourteen whites, including Narcissa and Marcus Whitman.

MARIE DORION

Pierre Dorion was hired as an interpreter for the 1811-12 overland expedition financed by John Jacob Astor and headed by Wilson Price Hunt. The purpose of the expedition was to establish a fur trading post at the mouth of the Columbia River.

Marie Dorion, Pierre's wife, was the only woman on the expedition. She brought her two sons, ages two and four, and was pregnant with her third child. At the headwaters of the Missouri River Pierre bought a horse from the Indians so Marie and the two children could ride. As the party approached the Blue Mountains Marie dropped out of the procession and on December 30, 1811 she gave birth. The following day she caught up to the party but the baby soon died and was buried beside the trail.

The expedition reached the mouth of the Columbia River on February 15, 1812. After recovering from their overland ordeal the Dorion family, along with several trappers, traveled east and set up a base camp at the mouth of the Boise River. Marie and the children stayed at the camp while the men began trapping. When Marie learned that a band of Bannocks was on the warpath she set out on horseback with her children to warn her husband and discovered he had been killed. Seeking refuge with friendly Indians along the Columbia River, she struggled to cross the Blue Mountains but was forced to make a winter camp. For the next fifty-three days she and her two sons existed on nothing but horsemeat and melted snow.

In the spring Marie led her children to a village of friendly Walla Walla Indians. A month later a group of trappers from Astoria took Marie and the children as far as Fort Okanogan. Eventually Marie married Jean Baptiste Toupin, a French-Canadian interpreter, and they settled in Oregon's Willamette Valley. Marie died in 1850.

FATHER OF THE EXODUS

Benjamin Singleton was a Tennessee-born slave. When he had the opportunity to escape he ran away and settled in Detroit, opening a boarding house and frequently sheltering other runaway slaves. After the Civil War and the passage of the 13th Amendment ending slavery, Singleton felt it was safe for him to return to Tennessee.

Singleton tried to purchase property in Tennessee, planning to give the land to former slaves; but the white landowners refused to sell to a black man. Undaunted, Singleton moved to Kansas where he platted a town and encouraged former slaves to move there by circulating advertising posters throughout the South. In response former slaves began an exodus from the South. The movement became known as the "Exodusters" and it reached its peak in 1879 when 50,000 former slaves exercised their newfound freedom to move to the western states.

The press referred to Singleton as the "Father of the Exodus" and in 1880 he was called to testify at Congressional hearings. He explained to the Congressmen that he was not the cause of the exodus, that the end of Reconstruction and the withdrawal of federal troops had allowed the South to return to racial oppression through segregation laws, and had given power to such hate groups as the Ku Klux Klan. Singleton maintained that his people were now afraid to live in the South.

Throughout his lifetime Singleton worked tirelessly for the African American community, believing their survival depended upon acquiring land and developing the financial resources to advance their own industries. Through his actions and dedication Benjamin Singleton was able to bring about fundamental social changes in the United States and to pass his vision on to future generations. He died in 1892.

BLOOD BROTHERS

Tom Jeffords was a miner, a scout and a deputy sheriff, but he is best remembered as the white man who became blood brothers with Cochise, the feared Apache warrior.

As a young man Cochise was unjustly accused of stealing cattle and abducting a child. An inexperienced Army officer ordered Cochise arrested and in the ensuing battle a soldier was killed and Cochise, suffering three bullet wounds, escaped. He retaliated by going on the warpath and for the next ten years Cochise and his followers conducted raids on military troops, settlers and traders. They were so effective that most outsiders withdrew from the region rather than risk being killed.

When Tom Jeffords became the superintendent of a pony express company he wanted to prevent his riders from being killed by the Indians. He rode alone into the mountains, located Cochise's camp and asked for safe passage for his mail riders. Cochise was so impressed with Jeffords's courage that he granted his request and eventually adopted the white man as his blood brother.

In 1871 General Oliver Howard was sent to end the Apache wars. He learned that the only white man Cochise trusted was Tom Jeffords and he enlisted Jeffords to help negotiate a peace treaty. A meeting was arranged and Cochise made two demands — that his followers be given a reservation in the Chiricahua Mountains and that Jeffords be assigned as the Indian agent. Both requests were granted and for several years there was peace. But the promises were broken. Jeffords was removed as the Indian agent and the Apaches were relocated to the San Carlos Reservation.

The last time the blood brothers saw each other Cochise asked Jeffords if he believed they would meet again in the afterlife. Jeffords said he thought so. The following day, June 8, 1874, Cochise died.

WOUNDED KNEE

The Lakota people were confined to their reservation without enough food to sustain them. A large group of Indians tried to leave but on December 29, 1890 soldiers surrounded their camp at Wounded Knee Creek.

According to the official report of commanding officer Colonel James Forsyth, the Indians were ordered to surrender all arms, but when a medicine man began the ghost dance and loudly proclaimed, "I have lived long enough," the soldiers became alarmed. It was claimed the Indians had rifles hidden under their blankets and that they suddenly cast off their blankets and began firing. Colonel Forsyth ordered his men to return fire. The Army declared the killings justified and promoted Colonel Forsyth to the rank of Major General. Three officers and fifteen enlisted men were awarded the Medal of Honor in what was officially called the "Battle of Wounded Knee Creek."

What the Army called a battle the Indians called a massacre. The Indians said that the soldiers took up commanding positions on hills overlooking the camp and began firing on the unarmed Indians. They even chased down women and children and killed them. And when a cease-fire was finally called the soldiers implored the survivors to come forward, telling them they would be safe, and then shot them down.

On New Year's Day a pit was dug and the frozen bodies of 146 Lakota men, women and children were thrown into a common grave. One member of the burial party remarked it was "a thing to melt the heart of a man, to see those little children thrown into the pit."

Wounded Knee became the final encounter of the bloody Indian wars of the 19th century. The grim truth remains that on that fateful day not a single hero emerged to change the course of history.

QUEEN OF THE WEST

She was born Lucille Wood Smith but for unknown reasons her parents soon changed her name to Frances Octavia. It was the first of what would be many name changes for the pretty girl from Texas. At the age of fourteen Frances eloped with an older classmate, Thomas Fox, and the child bride soon delivered a son. Thomas walked out on his family and Frances enrolled in secretarial school and married August Johns.

Frances was an aspiring singer. She found employment at a radio station and often sang at her desk. The station manager put her on the air and Frances went from singing secretary to a radio show regular. Her stage name was Dale Evans. She soon divorced August Johns and married Robert Butts.

A producer for 20th Century Fox "discovered" Dale Evans and Hollywood quickly repackaged her — shaving seven years off her age, requiring her to remove her wedding band and making up an elaborate story of her devotion to her teen-aged brother Tommy, who was actually her son. Dale appeared in a series of musicals before winning a starring role opposite Roy Rogers in a western movie.

Dale and Roy made several movies together but the popular co-stars suffered through personal tragedies. Roy lost his wife to post-natal complications and Dale's marriage ended in a bitter divorce in 1945. A year later the famous on-screen couple was married. Over the next fifty years they became the most recognized couple in the world, starring together in twenty-seven films and a long-running television show and recording more than 400 songs.

The couple had one child together, a daughter who died from complications of Downs Syndrome. This tragedy inspired Dale to write more than twenty books, donating the proceeds to charity. Dale Evans, the "Queen of the West," passed away peacefully in her sleep at the age of 88.

PART-TIME HERO

Henry Brown was a gambler, horse thief and gunman who gave up his outlaw life to become a hero to the citizens of Caldwell, Kansas. But in the end he reverted to his old ways and lost everything, including his life.

Brown drifted into Caldwell in July 1882 packing his two ivory-handled six-shooters. He volunteered for the recently vacated position of town marshal. The mayor informed Brown that the three previous marshals had all died in the line of duty. Brown simply shrugged his shoulders and said he could take care of himself. The mayor told him, "All right. It's your funeral."

Brown wasted no time in serving notice that he was the law in Caldwell. He killed one man for resisting arrest and another who foolishly challenged the marshal to a shootout. Word spread and Caldwell became a town the criminal element avoided. The citizens were so appreciative they presented Marshal Brown with a Winchester rifle elegantly engraved with the inscription, "For valuable services rendered the citizens of Caldwell."

To his credit Brown took the appreciation of the town to heart. He stopped drinking, gambling and gave up tobacco. He even proposed to a local woman, Maude Levagood, and bought a house after they were married. It appeared the outlaw had finally been tamed and settled down.

And then one morning in April 1884 four men attempted to rob the bank in the nearby settlement of Medicine Lodge. They were quickly apprehended. One of the men turned out to be Henry Brown. Nobody knows why he had given up so much to gain so little. In the end an angry mob hung three of the men. They told the unarmed Brown to run for it and then unceremoniously shot him in the back.

GOODNIGHT-LOVING

At the age of ten Charles Goodnight moved with his family from Illinois to Texas. By the time he was twenty he was involved in ranching and had accumulated a sizable herd of cattle that roamed the northwest Texas rangeland.

Goodnight believed in fighting for what he thought was right. He joined a local militia in their long-running battle against Comanche raiders and later became a member of the Texas Rangers. When the Civil War broke out he joined the Confederate forces, returning to Texas at the end of the war and undertaking a roundup of his cattle that had been left to roam on the open range during his absence.

Goodnight went in partnership with another rancher, Oliver Loving. They combined their cattle herds and decided to drive them across the deserts of west Texas to the new settlements in New Mexico and north to Colorado. They set out with a herd of 2,000 head, blazing a new trail from Belknap, Texas to Fort Sumner, New Mexico. This section became famous during the era of the cattle drives and was known as the Goodnight-Loving Trail.

The two men profited from their joint venture. Between them they pocketed more than $12,000 and immediately returned to Texas to assemble another herd of cattle. But Loving's financial success was short-lived. He died at the hands of renegade Comanches who attacked him on the trail in 1867. Goodnight, honoring Loving's dying request, delivered his partner's body for burial in Texas.

Over the next decade Goodnight extend his cattle drives as far as Granada, Colorado. In 1877 he went into partnership with John Adair, an investor, and they soon amassed a ranch that covered more than one million acres. Goodnight eventually sold his interest in the ranch and in his later years he dabbled in everything from mining to producing movies. He died in 1929.

SITTING BULL

Sitting Bull participated in his first battle, a raid against the neighboring Crow tribe, when he was fourteen years old. He soon realized the real enemy was the white invaders who killed the buffalo and stole Indian land.

About 1868 Sitting Bull became the head chief of the Lakota nation. His courage and bravery were legendary and it was said he had the ability to see into the future. When gold was discovered in the Black Hills of the Dakota Territory, Sitting Bull summoned more than 3,000 Lakota, Cheyenne and Arapaho to his camp along the Little Bighorn River. He told them of a dream he had in which he saw soldiers falling like grasshoppers from the sky.

On June 25, 1876 the Seventh Cavalry attacked the Indian camp and the soldiers, badly outnumbered, were forced to make a last stand on a nearby ridge. After this decisive battle Sitting Bull, fearing retaliation, led his band across the border into Canada and beyond the reach of the U. S. Army. But food was scarce in Canada and in 1881 Sitting Bull was forced to surrender.

Sitting Bull was held as a prisoner of war until he was allowed to join Buffalo Bill's Wild West show where he signed autographs and sold photographs of himself. After only four months he left the show and moved into a small cabin on the Lakota reservation. It was here that Sitting Bull had another vision — a meadowlark spoke to him, saying, "Your own people will kill you."

Amid growing fears that Sitting Bull would once again lead his people to war, government agents were sent to arrest him. Just before dawn on December 15, 1890 agents burst into Sitting Bull's cabin and dragged him outside. Tribal members had gathered to protect their chief and in the gun battle that followed Sitting Bull was shot and killed by one of the Lakota tribal policemen.

JOE MEEK

Joe Meek was born in Virginia in 1810. By the time he was nineteen years old he had signed on with William Sublette and for the next eleven years he trapped, traded and lived among the Indians.

In his later years Joe told many stories from this period of his life — his encounters with grizzly bears, fighting Indians, and tall tales that stretched a grain of truth to the edge of believability. During his years as a trapper Joe married two Indian women and when the era of the mountain man ended Joe began leading wagon trains of emigrants over the Oregon Trail. With his third wife, also an Indian, he finally settled on a donation land claim in the Willamette Valley. In 1843 he participated in the vote at Champoeg, campaigning to have the Oregon Country become part of the United States. At that meeting he was elected as the first Provisional sheriff and later served as a legislator.

Following the Whitman Massacre in 1847 Meek crossed the country in the dead of winter, suffering incredible hardships, before finally arriving in Washington and meeting with President James Polk. The Congress approved Oregon's territorial status on August 14, 1848 and President Polk appointed Meek marshal of the Oregon Territory. Serving in that capacity he presided over the hanging of five Indians who were implicated in the Whitman Massacre.

Toward the end of his life, as more and more settlers flooded into the Willamette Valley, Meek witnessed the stark reality of the changes that had swept over the West in a single generation. His half-breed children were systematically ostracized by the white society and by the time he died in 1875 few of the homesteaders felt there was a place in civilized Oregon for a man like the legendary mountain man, Joe Meek.

KIT CARSON

Christopher "Kit" Carson was born in Kentucky on Christmas Eve 1809. He was an infant when his family moved to a region called Upper Louisiana, which had been ceded to United States by France. When Kit was nine his father died and Kit spent his time hunting and trapping to provide food for his mother and nine brothers and sisters. At age sixteen he left home to forge a new life on the western frontier.

Kit was small in stature, standing five feet six and weighing only 140 pounds. He traveled the Santa Fe Trail and landed in Taos where he found employment as a cook, errand boy and harness repairman before hiring on with mountain man Ewing Young. Over the next twelve years Kit roamed the wilderness in the company of men like Young, Jim Bridger and Broken Hand Fitzpatrick. He explored the Rockies and the Sierra Nevada, crossed the Mojave Desert and the basin of the Great Salt Lake, traveled north to the drainage of the Snake and Columbia rivers and roamed as far south as Mexico.

During the summer of 1836 Kit took an Arapaho woman as his wife and she bore him a daughter they called Adaline. Two years later Kit's wife died and, needing a mother for Adaline, Kit married a Cheyenne woman. But that marriage was short-lived. On a trip to St. Louis, where Kit left Adaline with his sister so the young girl could attend school, Kit met John Fremont, a lieutenant with the Corps of Topographical Engineers. Fremont immediately hired Kit to lead an expedition across the Rocky Mountains.

Fremont, with Kit leading the way, made three expeditions to the West and wrote in glowing reports about his extraordinary guide, making Kit Carson a legend in his own time. When he died in 1868 flags were ordered to fly at half-mast.

NONSTOP

Four years after Charles Lindbergh electrified the world by flying nonstop across the Atlantic Ocean, Clyde Pangborn, an experienced daredevil from Wenatchee, Washington, and playboy Hugh Herndon, Jr., a novice flier, hoped to be the first to fly across the Pacific Ocean.

It was determined that even with a full load of fuel the plane chosen for the attempt did not have the necessary range. However, Pangborn had worked out a clever plan to reduce drag and soon after departing from Japan he put his plan into action, jettisoning the landing gear from the fuselage. The main structure fell away but the bracing rods remained. With the inexperienced Herndon at the controls Pangborn, battling 100-mile-per-hour wind and numbing cold, climbed outside the aircraft. He placed his feet on the wing strut, held on with one hand and used the other to remove the bolt from the bracing rod. When one side was free he climbed inside, warmed himself for a few minutes and repeated the procedure on the other bracing rod.

Without landing gear to slow the plane they climbed to 17,000 feet where they leveled off and picked up a steady tailwind. To save weight they had elected to fly without a radio or any survival equipment. They would either make the flight or die in the attempt.

An amateur radio operator on an Aleutian Island radioed that he had heard an airplane pass overhead but nothing more was known about the flight until a big red monoplane came roaring out of the sky at 7:14 a.m. on October 5, 1931, swooped low over the town of Wenatchee and belly-flopped onto the ground at the local airport. A cloud of dust momentarily obscured the plane and then it reappeared, teetered for a moment and fell onto its left wingtip. Pangborn and Herndon had become the first to fly nonstop across the Pacific Ocean.

JOHNNY APPLESEED

He was born John Chapman on September 26, 1774. Not much is known about his childhood but in later life a story about him appeared in *Harper's New Monthly Magazine* and he became a folk hero celebrated far and wide as Johnny Appleseed.

By all accounts Johnny Appleseed was a peculiar man. He had a strong belief that God would watch out for him and he walked around alone in the wilderness, among the Indians and wild beasts, and never carried a gun or a knife. He did not kill animals and subsisted on leaves, berries, fruit and bark. He walked barefooted, even in winter, rarely bathed, dressed in other people's castoff clothes and his hair and beard were long and unkempt.

Johnny Appleseed had a singular purpose in life. He felt that God had chosen him to distribute apple seeds across the land. When he found a suitable spot along the banks of a river or creek he cleared the area, planted his apple seeds and built a fence around the area so the seeds would be protected and could germinate and grow. He obtained seeds from cider mills and for more than forty years he traveled from Pennsylvania to the Great Lakes region, an estimated 10,000 square miles, sowing apple seeds.

But the influence of Johnny Appleseed reached a much wider area because on his travels he would stop wagon pioneers and hand them a small pouch filled with apple seeds. He told them, "Take this with you. Keep it out of the weather and when you get to where you're going, do me a favor and plant these seeds."

LAST STAND

George Armstrong Custer fought valiantly in the Civil War. When the war ended he sought, at all costs, to win fame fighting Indians on the western frontier. At the battle of the Little Bighorn he gave his life and in the process became an American hero.

On the morning of June 25, 1876 a large contingent of U.S. Army soldiers moved into position to attack a camp of Sioux and Cheyenne Indians camped along the Little Bighorn River. Lieutenant Colonel Custer, in command of the Seventh Cavalry, marched his forces along Rosebud Creek. All signs indicated a large camp of Indians directly ahead but Custer ignored the warning, just as he ignored the orders to wait for General Terry before beginning his attack. Instead Custer chose to split his regiment. Major Marcus Reno took 175 men south of the Indian encampment. Captain Frederick Benteen moved west with a force of 115 men, leaving Custer with 210 men. The pack train was to be guarded by the remaining 135 men.

Reno's battalion started down the valley in columns, first at a trot and then galloping. The Indians counterattacked and routed Reno's men. When Benteen joined the battle Custer and his men were left alone to face more than one thousand warriors. Although Custer and his soldiers fought bravely they were all dead in less than an hour. It took two long days before General Terry could rescue the troops led by Reno and Benteen.

The public heralded Custer as a hero and Custer's Last Stand became the rallying point of the Indian wars. Over the next decade recruits, who often referred to themselves as "Custer Avengers", punished the Indians. Never again were the Indians able to amass a force as large as they had at the battle of the Little Bighorn.

Rick Steber's Tales of the Wild West Series is available in hardbound and paperback books featuring illustrations by Don Gray. Current titles in the series include:

OREGON TRAIL Vol. 1
PACIFIC COAST Vol. 2
INDIANS Vol. 3
COWBOYS Vol. 4
WOMEN OF THE WEST Vol. 5
CHILDREN'S STORIES Vol. 6
LOGGERS Vol. 7
MOUNTAIN MEN Vol. 8
MINERS Vol. 9
GRANDPA'S STORIES Vol. 10
PIONEERS Vol. 11
CAMPFIRE STORIES Vol. 12
TALL TALES Vol. 13
GUNFIGHTERS Vol. 14
GRANDMA'S STORIES Vol. 15
WESTERN HEROES Vol. 16

Other books written by Rick Steber —
NO END IN SIGHT   *HEARTWOOD*
BUY THE CHIEF A CADILLAC *ROUNDUP*
BUCKAROO HEART   *LAST OF THE PIONEERS*
NEW YORK TO NOME   *TRACES*
WILD HORSE RIDER   *RENDEZVOUS*

If unavailable at local retailers, write directly to the publisher for a free catalog.

Bonanza Publishing
Box 204
Prineville, Oregon 97754